OUR GUEST BOOK

www.ingramcontent.com/pod-product-compliance
Lightning Source LLC
Chambersburg PA
CBHW041546260326
41914CB00016B/1561
9781733327282